# SPIRIT WORDZ

## BY
## BOKHABINYANA
## RADIANCE LOVELIGHT

**EDITING,
COMMENTARY & PHOTOGRAPHY
BY
BOKHABINYANA
RADIANCE LOVELIGHT
&
JUDAH JAH LOVE**

***LOVELIGHT*
Publications ©**

# BOKHABINYANA
## (RADIANCE LOVELIGHT)

∞ - 30/12/85 - 9/5/16 - ∞

***LOVELIGHT***
**Publications ©**

**ISBN** 978-1-9997018-9-5

# CONTENTS

# SPIRIT WORDZ

To My Spirit of Light (KARA BOPHELO ASHENAFI ABREY)
To My Spirit of Love (STUART JUDAH JAH LOVE ABREY)
& To The Spirit of LoveLight within All Living Beings
May the Spirit Inside the Words in this book Inspire you
to
Say what u r born to say,
to do what u r born to do & to Live True to the Highest in you!
From My ❤ to your ❤ ~ 1 eternal ❤

# INTRODUCTION

"SPIRIT WORDZ" is a collection of poetry written by my Wife, "Bokhabinyana" (Khabi), which means "Radiance", in Her mother-tongue, Setswana. Born on 30/12/85, She grew up in Meadowlands, Soweto, South Africa. We met in the UK on 9/5/08 and two years, two days later, on 11/5/10, we got married in Jo'berg. Tragically though, back in the UK, on our eighth anniversary of meeting, at eight months pregnant, Khabi died from an arson attack on our home by a mentally-ill neighbour. She was just 3o years young.

When this happened my inner sun went down, but I know life and love are eternal, so I try to remind myself that, like the sun at night, She is only gone from sight; that where She is, She is still shining bright, still alive and absolutely free and safe, along with our beautiful Daughter, KaRa; refer to "Tribute To The Infinite Ones"and "& Then Fear Happened...", where Khabi reminds us that death is a growth into higher meditations. She always used to say, "EVERYTHING HAPPENS THE WAY GOD WANTED IT TO HAPPEN." We should try to remember this sentiment.

Khabi was always writing (and *still is*, in the spirit dimension, see P.66 of my book on eternal life, "THE COMFORTER", where evidence of this is documented). She finished compiling "SPIRIT WORDZ" just days before the fire. She signed all Her poems as Bokhabinyana (Radiance LoveLight) and "LoveLight" really does describe Her Spirit, presence and smile perfectly. She is pure sunshine and I stand in awe of Her brilliance and vision as I do my best to present and promote Her essential messages, which lead humanity to the re-discovery of its true Identity, purpose and destiny. Khabi's delicate voice must not be silenced, Her Light of Love must eternally SHINE!

These final versions of the poems are set out in the order of the contents page that Khabi had already completed. They are also presented in the fonts She had chosen, which reflect many of the poems themes. Most of the pictures were chosen by Khabi specifically for "SPIRIT WORDZ." Khabi has also written explanations for some of the poems and I've written brief explanations for others. I have also added some comments, translations & pronunciations in square brackets. Khabi often spells "thanks" as "th<u>ankh</u>s", using the Egyptian word for "life" - "ankh", implying giving thanks for life. The last two poems are incomplete, but what is there is too poignant and meaningful to be omitted.

"SPIRIT WORDZ" is a beautiful mixture of enlightened guidance, 3<sup>rd</sup>-eye-opening revelations, undeniable prophecy & heart-felt honesty & openness, sharing with us Her most personal thoughts and experiences in such a touching way. Here is a window into the life and Mind of a true, living Angel, revealing a beautiful & unique Soul Who has left us with essential messages of Radiant Love-Light, guiding us through this mechanical and often painful life.

THANK YOU, MY ANGEL-QUEEN! X

Judah JAH Love<br>July 1<sup>st</sup>, 2016

NB. I have used capitals in reference to Khabi as Her *Spirit* has not died, only Her *body* has; Her Spirit has become One with the Divine Source of Life, making Her truly Divine also.

# TRIBUTE TO THE INFINITE ONES

YOUR TIMELESS WORDS ARE ALL I HAD
TO GUIDE ME THRU THE GOOD AND THE BAD
LIFTING ME UP WHEN I'M FEELING SAD
AS I WALK THROUGH LIFE WITH MY WRITING PAD
THEY'VE KEPT ME FAR FROM GOING MAD

YOUR MYSTICAL THOUGHTS ARE ALL I POSSESS
THEY'VE DRAGGED ME OUT OF MENTAL DISTRESS
YOU TAUGHT ME NEVER TO SETTLE FOR LESS
THAN THE HEIGHTS OF SPIRITUAL PROGRESS
BY FOLLOWING THE PATH OF CONSCIOUSNESS
NURTURING THE HEART WITH SOULFULLNESS
ANCIENT WORDS FOREVER RELEVANT

OPENING MY THIRD EYE
TO THE DIVERSE UNIVERSE
REVEALING THE LIGHT OF HUMANITY'S DIVINITY
REMINDING ME TO LIVE WITH BOTHO: THE ART OF SOLIDARITY
MANIFESTING UBUNTU: THE SPIRIT OF INTEGRITY
YOUR WORDS ARE TO ME THE COSMIC DRUM BEAT
LIKE SACRED PRECEPTS FREE FROM CONCEIT
WORDS OF PURITY SAFELY STORED IN MY HEARTDRIVE
WHERE THE BLOOD IN MY VEINS KEEPS THEM ALIVE

YOUR SILENT TEACHINGS CONSTANTLY CHALLENGE MY
PERCEPTION
& INSPIRE ME TO PAY CAREFULL ATTENTION TO MY EVERY
INTENTION
AND WHEN I'M LED ASTRAY, YOUR WORDS IN ME GIVE ME
DIRECTION
& FIRM CORRECTION

EVEN IN THESE TIMES OF BRUTALITY N VANITY
YOUR WORDS GIVE ME THE GIFT OF CLARITY
YOUR WORDS HOLD THE ULTIMATE SOLUTION
TO SET ME FREE FROM ANY STATE OF ILLUSION
LEADING THE WAY TO HIGHER INSIGHT
OF LOVE BEING THE SUPREME GUIDING LIGHT

YOUR WORDS SPEAK OF IMMORTALITY
TUNING ME INTO THE FREQUENCY OF ETERNITY
WHEREIN REIGNS PEACE N TRANQUILITY
I PAY TRIBUTE TO YOUR INFINITE WORDS OF KINDNESS
AFFIRMING THE STATE OF OUR
SACRED ONENESS BY LEARNING TO HARNESS
THE GIFT OF LOVE
THE TOTALITY OF ALL REALITY
I PAY TRIBUTE TO THE ONES GONE BEFORE ME SOARING THE
INFINITE GALAXY


[Botho is pronounced, "Boh-tu" and Ubuntu, "Uboontu"]

# TRIBUTE TO THE INFINITE ONES – EXPLANATION:

1 ORIGINALLY WROTE THIS POEM TO THANKH:
MY GRANDMOTHER
"MAWE"
NELLY MAMATLALA MABE-PULUMO:

FOR LOVING, NURTURING
AND SHOWERING ME WITH AFFECTION.
FOR INVESTING TIME IN TEACHING ME THE SPIRITUAL PRINCIPLES
THAT HAVE GUIDED ME THROUGH LIFE AND ULTIMATELY
STRENGTHENED ME THROUGH MY PERSONAL JOURNEY.
HER WORDS ARE MY PRICELESS INHERITENCE.
1 CHERISH HER TIMELESS SENSE OF HUMOUR, HER STERNNESS
WHEN NEEDED AND HER WISDOM.
1 STAND STRONG IN HER STRENGTH & HER PRAYERS.

TO "MMABONE"
BOKHABINYANA JOSEPHINE MABE:

KEA LEBOGA MOKWENA* FOR ALL THE TEACHINGS YOU LEFT
BEHIND TO BE PASSED ON TO ME AND FOR CARRYING YOURSELF
WITH DIGNITY.

TO "BABA" A.K.A. "DA CHIEF"
WILSON DUMISANI NDEBELE:

FOR CHOOSING TO BE MY DAD & MAKING PROVISION FOR MY
EDUCATION, MY LIVELIHOOD AND HELPING ME TO FULFILL MY
DREAM OF TRAVELLING.
NGIYABONGA BABA


*thank you to you of the Crocodile Clan

# TO THE SPIRIT OF "RICKY"
## RICHARD ABREY:

THANKH YOU FOR BEING & FOR LEAVING THE PUREST, MOST
BEAUTIFUL PART OF YOU IN YOUR SON.

1 GIVE HONOUR TO ALL THE INFINITE LIGHT BEINGS
* MY ANCESTORS *
* KINDRED SPIRITS *  WHO WALKED BEFORE ME & ARE NOW
SOARING THE INFINITE LIGHT GALAXY.
1 GIVE THANKHS, FOR YOUR WORDS ARE MY GUIDANCE,
INSPIRATION, COMFORT, CORRECTION AND STRENGTH THROUGH
MY JOURNEY IN THE WORLD OF TIME.

BLESSINGS TO YOU DEAR HEARTS

CHRIST
BUDDHA
LAO TZU
PARAMAHANSA YOGANANDA
HAILE SELASSIE 1
BOB MARLEY
KAHLIL GIBRAN
MUMMY (NO SHAKING)

# RISING PHOENIX

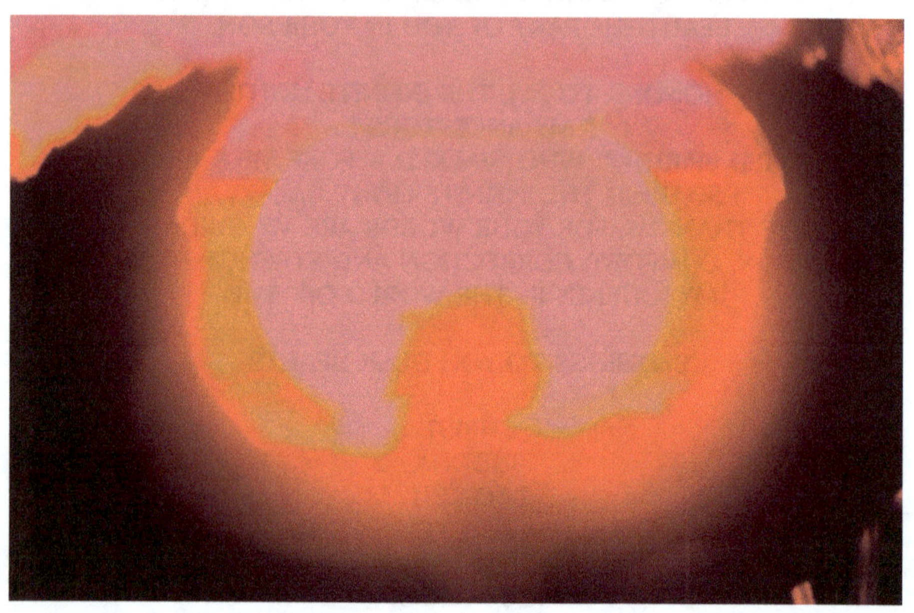

Like the phoenix I rise wise
Free from mental shackles & ties
Lifted by the silence within I self
I rise from the ashes
Empowered & wholly restored
Healed and complete
Unsinged like Shadrach, Meschach n Abednego
I rise from the burning flames of fear and illusion
Revived & ready to accept, receive & appropriate
The Priceless Gift of Love
I rise to greet the dawning of cosmic insight
Free to bask in the purity of unspeakable bliss

Clothed in humility
The honour of evolving humanity
Rescued by integrity
Emerging from deep within the refining fire
I rise from the ashes - lifted on the wings of Pure Being

I rise like the phoenix
Leaving behind the inner wars
I once waged against I self
I have passed through the door of Truth
I am the consciousness of the galaxies
And the timeless seas
I rise with fire in I soul
I am Divine Light
I pre-exist time
One with the entire cosmos and beyond
The heart of the earth
ONE with the ALL
Omniscient
Omnipotent
Omnipresent
Great Allmighty Oversoul of the diverse universe
I AM that I AM
Radiant like the Beaming SunRise
I rise to greet the dawning
Of Infinite Love & Infinite Light -
The Beauty of Eternal Day

# RISING PHOENIX

- commentary by Judah JAH Love:

Khabi was finishing compiling "SPIRIT WORDZ" just before She left the physical world and entered into the Eternal-Love-Light-Life, when Her body died from inhaling smoke caused by a fire set deliberately outside our door by a mentally-ill neighbour. So it was quite shocking to read a poem about rising out of a fire. I mean, She'd read it to me before, but since these tragic events took place, it has taken on new significance and poignancy.

One could argue that the poem's not speaking literally, but I'm quite sure that, here at least, where She uses the word "restored", She is using a term for death that I use in my book, "The Comforter", where I say that when the body dies, the spirit becomes "Restored In Perfection" - "R.I.P."

Poetic & Prophetic!

Khabi was named after Her Great GrandMother, Bokhabinyana Josephine, as Her Granny said of Her when She was a baby, "This is my Mum!" The sheer insight and depth of Khabi's messages lead me to believe this could well be true.

# MY PERSONAL AWAKENING: REBIRTH

Once I was Hedged in
Tossed to and fro by unfavourable circumstances
Plagued by struggles and troubles
Tormented by fear
Dangling helplessly at the bottom of the food chain
Not sure how much more I could take of the strain
Distressed n depressed
Sick and tired of being sick and tired
Left questioning how I could end the awful nightmare
Suddenly...
My eyes are open to see
That I alone hold the power to set myself free
The key is in me
I've had it along
The ability to sing a new song
And take responsibility for where I went wrong
I'm blessed with the gift of a new perspective
By consciously filling my mind with positive
Thoughts of love, peace and greater possibility
I begin to slowly drain out
The endless stream of self-inflicted negativity
The struggle has ceased
The pain is erased
Ushered into internal rest n total restoration
Escorted into the presence of pure being
By unconditional love

Wait...
Is this really me?
Finally free

Words of light fill my once afflicted mind
I'm in a place of tranquillity
I pinch myself
Am I hallucinating?
Just a second in doubt I almost slip back
I'm gracefully enabled
To comprehend this overwhelming experience
While in the midst of the Silence...
A voice from deep within whispers gently
You have finally woken up from the illusion
It was all a large mirage.
Still intrigued by the all so rapid winds of change
I continue to listen silently, the voice speaks on
There is nothing strange - you chose the change
Its simply that simple!!!
The nightmare exists only in thinking
Heaven n hell r states of mind
Free will is a gift given to all mankind
The chaos serves as an alarm to awaken you
To what you know in your heart is true
Take your light and wake others up
To the reality of their liberty
Wake them up from that dreadful dream
Into the joy and wholeness of their Divinity

# BORN TO SHINE

YES YOUR LIFE IS DIVINE
NOW IS ALWAYS THE RIGHT TIME
TO FOLLOW YOUR PATHLINE
DON'T UNDERMINE YOUR UNIQUE DESIGN
THERE IS SOLID PROOF
IN VALIDATING YOUR INNERMOST TRUTH
THE MORE YOU GIVE THE BETTER YOU LIVE
YOUR RADIANT LIGHT
IS INVALUABLE IN THE MOST HIGH'S SIGHT

THE BOOK OF LIFE IS WRITTEN IN YOUR SOUL
INVEST TIME IN MANIFESTING YOUR SACRED ROLE
THERE IS NO MEASURE TO YOUR INNATE TREASURE
WHY COMPETE WHEN YOU ARE COMPLETE?
YOUR JOURNEY THRU TIME IS A BIG DEAL
INTEGRITY IS YOUR ETERNAL SEAL
YOUR HONEST EXPRESSION GIVES INSPIRATION
AND LEAVES A POSITIVE, TIMELESS IMPRESSION
YOUR GIFT
IS THE ANSWER TO THE CRIES OF MANKIND
YOUR MOTIVATION CAN RESTORE PEACE OF MIND
DON'T WASTE YOUR LIFE IN AIMLESS HASTE
YOU ARE THE SEED FOR THE NEW EARTH
A SPECIAL STAR
WAS CHOSEN TO ANNOUNCE YOUR BIRTH
KNOW YOUR TRUE WORTH
YOUR VOICE
CAUSES THE ENTIRE COSMOS TO REJOICE
YOU HAIL FROM THE KINGDOM OF INFINITE WISDOM
YOU STEM FROM A SUPERNATURAL RACE
LAVISHED WITH UNLIMITED GRACE
FLOWING FROM THE INFINITE FOUNTAIN OF SUPPLY
YOU WERE BORN TO GROW, EXPAND & MULTIPLY
YOU ARE BORN TO SHINE
YES YOUR LIFE IS DIVINE
NOW IS ALWAYS THE RIGHT TIME
TO FOLLOW YOUR UNIQUE PATHLINE
SAY WHAT YOU WERE BORN TO SAY
NEVER EVER HIDE YOUR LIGHT AWAY

# SHADOW ME
### (MYSTERY IN A SIMPLE SMILE)

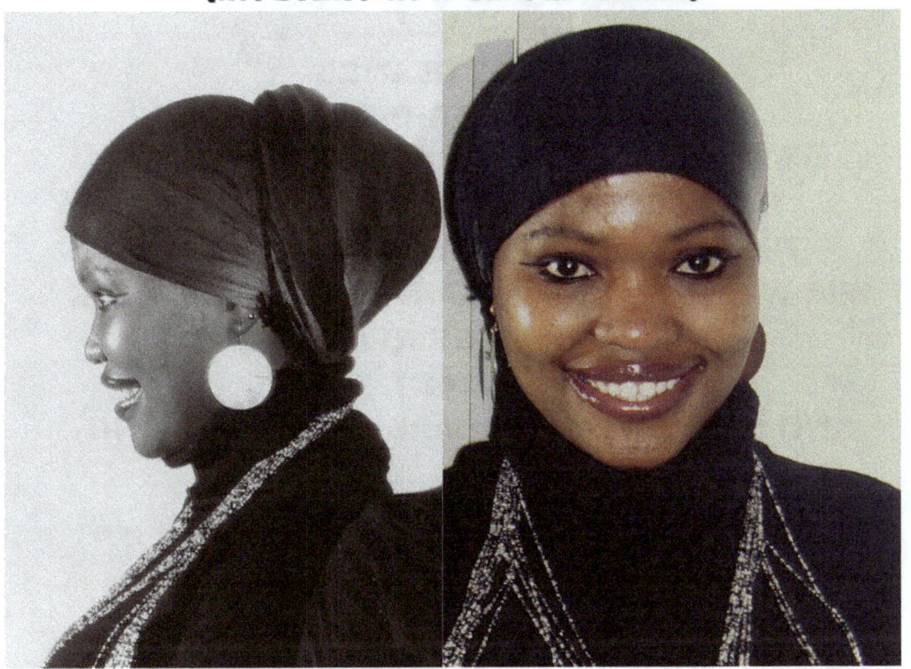

A DARK PRESENCE WALKED CLOSELY WITH ME
SHE DIDN'T SAY A WORD
YET I HEARD HER EVERY THOUGHT
THOUGHTS OF BEWILDERMENT
& UNEXPLAINED SADNESS
THOUGHTS OF FEAR AND SELF DOUBT
THOUGHTS OF DESPAIR
THOUGHTS AS DARK AS HER PRESENCE
SHE FOLLOWED ME CLOSELY
SHE SEEMED SO ISOLATED
& DETATCHED FROM MY REALITY

SHE WAS LOST IN HER OWN DARKNESS
SO EAGER TO REACH OUT
BUT AFRAID OF REJECTION

AT FIRST GLANCE
HER DARKNESS FRIGHTENED ME
IT SEEMED TO OVERSHADOW MY LIGHT
THE CLOSER I MOVED TOWARDS HER
THE MORE I FELT HER UNSPOKEN PAIN
SHE WAS TRYING TO REPRESS HER EMOTIONS
OF UNEXPRESSED ANGER,
NEGLECT
AND SHAME FOR HER DARK STATE OF BEING

YET HER EYES GAVE HER AWAY
HER SOUL WAS NAKED & UNHIDDEN
IT REFLECTED ITSELF
IN HER LONELINESS AND VULNERABILITY
SHE FELT POVERTY
HAD STRIPPED HER OF HER DIGNITY
SHE WAS UNCONSCIOUS OF HER DIVINITY
AFRAID TO LOVE
AFRAID TO BE LOVED

HER BAGGAGE SEEMED UNNECESSARILY HEAVY
SHE CARRIED MORE THAN SHE NEEDED
I QUESTIONED MY OWN INVOLVEMENT IN HER
JOURNEY
AFTERALL WHO WAS I TO JUDGE?
WHY HAD THIS FIGURE CHOSEN
TO WALK SO CLOSE TO ME?

I WANTED TO ASK  HER
BUT I DIDN'T WANT TO HURT HER
I COULD SENSE MY OWN EGO'S LONGING
TO PLAY THE ROLE OF A HERO
BY RESCUING HER FROM HER WALLOWING SELF

INSTEAD I CHOSE TO WALK ALONG
SILENTLY OBSERVING HER EVERY MOVE
I ALSO FELT A NEED
TO COMPLETELY BLOCK HER OUT
TO PRETEND I HADN'T NOTICED HER
TO WALK FASTER
TO MAKE A QUICK AND SWIFT ESCAPE
AFTERALL JUST LOOKING AT HER
SEEMED TO BE SAPPING MY ENERGY

YET
THE MORE I OBSERVED HER
THE MORE I FELT
I WAS GETTING TO INNERSTAND HER
ALTHOUGH SHE DIDN'T SAY A WORD
I FELT BAD FOR JUDGING HER
WITHOUT REALLY KNOWING HER
SO I SMILED AT HER
SHE STARED AT ME WITH A KIND OF
KNOWINGNESS
THAT I COULDN'T QUITE EXPLAIN
I RECOGNIZED A GLIMSPE
OF FAMILIARITY IN HER EYES

I SMILED AGAIN
THIS TIME IT FELT LIKE I WAS LOOKING INTO MY
OWN  EYES
SHE WEPT
I SAW MYSELF IN HER
AS HER DARKNESS SLOWLY FADED
IT WAS AS IF I WAS LOOKING IN A MIRROR –

HER MANNERISMS, HER SUDDEN SPARK
HER IMMEDIATE RESPONSE TO KINDNESS
I WAS QUICKLY REALISING
JUST HOW MUCH SHE HAD REFLECTED MY OWN
FEARS,
INSECURITIES & DARKNESS

SHE WAS MY VERY OWN SHADOW
THAT'S WHY SHE CHOSE TO WALK SO CLOSE TO
ME
& BASICALLY A SIMPLE SMILE HAD SET HER FREE
MY LIGHT WAS SHINING OUT OF DARKNESS
AND THE DARKNESS COULD NOT COMPREHEND IT

FOR THE FIRST TIME EVER
I WAS AT HOME WITH BOTH SIDES OF ME.
ENABLED TO LOVE AND TO BE LOVED
I HAD WALKED A MILE IN THE JOURNEY OF TIME
STRENGTHENED BY THE MYSTERY
OF MY OWN SIMPLE SMILE.

# SHADOW ME – EXPLANATION:

## ADDRESS, ACCEPT
## & EMBRACE YOUR SHADOWS

DURING MY JOURNEY OF INVOLUTION (INNER STANDING) I FOUND  ASPECTS OF MYSELF THAT ARE CHALLENGING TO DEAL WITH AND DIFFICULT TO ACCEPT.

A SHADOW IS AN AREA OF DARKNESS CREATED WHEN A SOURCE OF LIGHT IS BLOCKED.

I WROTE THIS POEM WHEN I CAME FACE TO FACE WITH MY OWN SHADOWS OF FEAR, SHADOWS OF SELF DOUBT, SHADOWS OF INSECURITY, SHADOWS OF ISOLATION, SHADOWS OF PAST HURTS AND ALL THE DARK AREAS WITHIN MY OWN THOUGHTS THAT WERE BLOCKING MY INNER LIGHT SOURCE.

MY FIRST APPROACH TO THESE PARTS OF MYSELF WAS TO SHUN THEM, REPRESS THEM AND PRETEND THEY DIDN'T EXIST. AS I WALKED FURTHER INTO MY SPIRITUAL PATH I REALISED I HAD TO OBSERVE EVERY ASPECT OF MYSELF IN ORDER TO TRULY KNOW AND FULLY ACCEPT MYSELF. NEEDLESS TO SAY IT WAS EASY TO EMBRACE THE BEAUTIFUL, VIBRANT, GLOWING, POSITIVE PARTS OF ME. THE REAL HARD SHIP TO SAIL WAS SEEING THE PARTS OF ME THAT WERE NOT ALL THAT GRACIOUS: THE DARK THOUGHTS OF JUDGEMENT, SELF DOUBT &

SOUR MEMORIES THAT I SEEMED TO CLING TO IN ORDER TO
JUSTIFY UNJUST BEHAVIOUR. MY BLAME GAME TACTICS THAT AVERTED ME OF RESPONSIBILTY FOR MY MISTAKES.

MY SHADOW WAS MY TEACHER, SHE TAUGHT ME HOW TO BE TRULY PRESENT AND HONEST WITH ME. SHE WALKED CLOSELY WITH ME & GAVE ME THE GIFT OF SELF ACCEPTANCE & FORGIVENESS. SHE ALLOWED ME TO OBSERVE MY SUBCONSCIOUS DISPLAYS OF SOPPINESS, DEPRESSION, REPRESSION AND THE NOT SO EASY TO ADMIT ACTS OF HOLIER THAN THOU, FINGER POINTING TRICKS.

SHE TAUGHT ME TO OBSERVE THE SHADOWS SURROUNDING MY INTENTIONS, MY WORDS AND MY DEEDS. SHE HELD ME ACCOUNTABLE TO ME, REMINDING ME THAT THE JUDGEMENT I PLACED ON OTHERS WAS A REFLECTION OF THE DARKNESS I WAS AVOIDING TO FACE IN ME. MY LIGHT INTRODUCED ME TO MY SHADOW FOR LIGHT SHINES OUT OF DARKNESS AND DARKNESS CANNOT COMPREHEND IT.

JUST AS I COULDN'T RUN AWAY FROM MYSELF, I COULDN'T RUN AWAY FROM MY SHADOW.

BECAUSE OF MY SHADOW I AM ABLE TO LOVE & EMBRACE THE COMPLEXITY THAT IS ME WITHOUT THE NEED TO DEMONIZE MY FLAWS. FACING MY WEAKNESS WITHOUT HIDING BEHIND

MY STRENGTH. I AM RESPONSIBLE FOR MY ACTIONS AND REACTIONS, RESPONSIBLE FOR RESOLVING MY OWN INNER CONFLICTS.

OUR JOURNEY IN TIME IS ABOUT LOVING OTHERS AS WE LOVE OURSELVES SO IT STANDS THAT WE MUST FIRST LEARN TO LOVE OURSELVES.

QUOTE:
BY OWNING YOUR SHADOW, YOU EMBRACE YOUR FULL HUMANITY. EVEN THOSE WHO R DEEPLY SPIRITUAL GO THRU DARK NIGHTS WHEN DEPRESSION AND NOT KNOWING TAKE ON TERRIFYING DIMENSIONS. EVEN NATURE, THE SOURCE OF INSPIRATION HAS ITS SHADOW ELEMENTS
HURRICANES, VOLCANIC ERUPTIONS, FLOODS.
- FREDERIC & MARY ANN BRUSSAT

# STILL IN THE SILENCE
## *(RISING ABOVE ARGUMENTS)*

Misunderstandings & useless ramblings
causing an unnecessary fight
Everyone's out to prove that they're right
ignoring the warnings of divine insight
As the good vibe's fading
a negative vibe's quickly invading
Egos rushing at full speed
not at all aware there is no need
to proceed in sowing this bitter seed
No one's listening to what the other has to say
everyone's going astray
to defend their own way

Drag your self out if you must
coz
at all times love must reign n prevail

Rise
time to be wise
take a breath and realise
that controlling your reactions
is just as important as controlling your actions
Real truth is its own proof
step into the silence
escape the verbal violence
Silence is free from malice it never reflects unkindness
trust its calmness to restore all oneness
Too much talk is selfishness
just a recipe for more distress

Think,
don't allow your morals to sink

We become a part of what we impart
and live thru the karmic consequences
of any experiences
we put others thru

Stay true to the silence in you
so slow down your pace -
step into that divine place
honour your sacred space
embrace the peace
that comes from quiet release
by stepping into the chamber of silence
this way u have surely passed
the mortal ego test
by simply allowing your mouth to rest
you've been mature enough
to listen and appreciate
the lessons only learnt
when you are
**STILL IN THE SILENCE**

# STILL IN  THE SILENCE
## – EXPLANATION:

This is a poem I wrote almost immediately after I'd dragged myself out of an argument, which at that time was something extremely hard for me to do because I was so accustomed to having the last say.

I had recently made a pact with myself to get over myself, so I took my stroppy self out of the situation onto the naughty step, well I went into the bedroom with the intention to sulk in an attempt to win over an undeserved apology that would  massage my bruised ego
(adults are just big kids).

So this is the poem that came to me during time-out while I was about to start feeling sorry for myself and find reasons to justify unleashing my verbal weapons of mass destruction on my dear husband.

# DEAR FALSEHOOD

*FALSEHOOD IMPLIES ALL LOWER-SELF FEARS, LIES, DELUSIONS & FABRICATIONS THAT DRAG US INTO THE GAME OF ILLUSION - FORCING US TO THINK WE R SEPERATE N ALONE WHEN WE ARE ACTUALLY ONE COMPLETE WHOLE...*

DEAR FALSEHOOD

IT'S TIME TO LET YOU GO
IT'S FINALLY TIME FOR YOU TO DIE
THERE ARE SO MANY REASONS WHY
FIRSTLY YOU MADE ME LIVE A LIE
YOU BRUISED MY WINGS
AND TOLD ME THAT I COULD NEVER FLY
THIS TIME AROUND YOU WONT SEE ME CRY
B'COZ TODAY IS THE DAY I SAY GOOD BYE!!!

I CAN'T BELIEVE IT'S TAKEN ME SO LONG
TO REALIZE YOU'VE DONE ME WRONG
YOU'VE ALWAYS BEEN AGAINST THE HIGHER ME
THAT THE ALLMIGHTY SPIRIT CREATED ME TO BE
YOU'VE NEVER WANTED ME TO BE FREE
THIS IS YET ANOTHER REASON WHY I HAVE TO LET YOU GO
YOU JUST WOULDN'T LET ME GROW

NOW YOUR PART IN MY STORY IS OVER
FOR YEARS YOU TURNED ME INTO A MENTAL SLAVE
BRINGING ME SHAME AND MAKING ME BEAR THE BLAME
ALWAYS MAKING ME AFRAID & FILLING ME WITH FALSE PRIDE
FOR A WHILE I BELIEVED
I COULDN'T TAKE THINGS IN MY OWN STRIDE
I WISH I'D KNOWN
U WERE JUST TRYING TO TAKE OVER MY MIND

ANXIOUS OVER THINKING NEGATIVE OVERDRIVE
STRIVING BUT NEVER ARRIVING
THIS IS WHY I'M GLAD TO SAY GOOD BYE
I'M NOT INTERESTED IN PLAYING YOUR LAME GAMES
I REFUSE TO GIVE YOU THE POWER TO DRIVE ME INSANE

ALL MY LIFE I SEARCHED HIGH N LOW
TRYING TO LOCATE THE ENEMY OF MY SOUL
ONLY TO FIND YOUR FALSENESS FILLING THAT ROLE
DISTRACTING ME FROM THE TRUTH OF MY WHOLENESS
& FROM BEARING THE FRUITS OF SOULFULNESS
KEEPING ME FROM ACKNOWLEDGING
MY SACRED ONENESS WITH ALL EARTHLINGS
PREVENTING ME FROM EXPRESSING THE LIGHT OF MY IDENTITY
– MY CREATIVE INTEGRITY –
MY PATH OF AWAKENING ALL
TO THE DIVINITY HIDDEN WITHIN THEIR HUMANITY


SO NOW IT'S TIME TO LET YOU DIE
COZ YOU MADE ME LIVE A LIE
MADE ME THINK I WOULD NEVER FLY
SO AWAY WITH YOUR DECEPTIONS, MISCONCEPTIONS,
CONDEMNATIONS, ISOLATIONS & SEGREGATIONS
NO MORE WILL I ALLOW YOU TO HINDER MY FLOW
NO MORE WILL I LET YOU CRAMP MY STYLE & DIM MY SHINE
I REFUSE TO DROWN IN YOUR LIE –
TODAY I BOLDLY BID YOU GOODBYE!

# ONLY YOU

ONLY YOU
Hold within you the healing, the remedy and the cure to
whatever it is that ails your soul
You need no ones approval and no one to permit you
to fully be
The following prescription is on me
Completely free:

Accept yourself
Be at home with your own being
Own the confidence to take your dreams seriously
This is a journey of self discovery
Walk in your destiny
No one can be you for you
Your consciousness depends on you
The lessons you learn within become your conduct
You possess the key to your own progress

There are people
ONLY YOU
Can reach!!!
There are countless life altering lessons
ONLY YOU
Can teach

You were born complete, there's no need to compete
Leave the past in the past, don't put your life
on constant repeat

ONLY YOU
Can change the mind numbing

"Much the same - can't complain -
Same shit, different day" syndrome.
Don't live to moan n groan
Don't spend your time waiting for validation
That is the surest route to stagnation
Follow your inner motivation
The universe will fund and back your inspirations
Allmighty Spirit guides n provides
Ride your own tide
Unlimited Possibilities n Countless Opportunities
Are in every breath you take
There are changes & differences
ONLY YOU
Can make
There's way too much at stake
Always live true to the highest in you
For loves sake
Walking your journey of truth is your gift to the Divine
You are a one-off design
Master yourself - coz
ONLY YOU
Can fully be yourself

Being kind is the simplest way to be who you really are
Have no fear
Coz there's no danger of failure in simply being
Only lessons in the experience
Of gathering knowledge of self wisdom
In the university of you

Remember
Once u awake u automatically graduate
Your conscience cannot fall back
Into the sleep of ignorance

Know that the Creator God n Goddess live within you
Stop struggling to be who u already are
You are a unique light being
Don't tranquillize yourself
With material vanity
Live with sincerity
Love deeply
The entire cosmos celebrates your being
Your star beams bright throughout the galaxy
You are not just matter
You are infinite Spirit at Her best
And you matter

ONLY YOU
Can look within and see your divinity as complete reality

ONLY YOU
Can live your truth deeply without apology

The whole earth travails like a woman in labour – Awaiting
Your special gift
That's designed and created to inspire n uplift
The entire planet's love light energy
And restore humanity's synchronicity
With all that was, all that is and all that ever will be.

ONLY YOU
Can succeed at being
TRUE TO THE HIGHEST IN YOU

# I HAD A VISION OF OUR TRUE ORIGIN. . .

AS A NATURALLY SPIRITUAL CIVILIZATION
A PEOPLE OF PEACE & CONSCIOUS MEDITATION
WITH ROCK SOLID FAITH IN TIMES OF TRIBULATION
A NATION CHARACTERIZED BY ONENESS
– NO SEPERATION –
RICH IN LOVE AND POSITIVE VIBRATIONS
TEACHING THE ART OF THE HEART
THE VITAL KEY TO SELF REALIZATION
SOARING TO NEW DIMENSIONS OF SOULFULL EVOLUTION
EXPERIENCING WISDOM
THE HIGHEST FORMS OF ILLUMINATION
A KINGDOM ABOUNDING IN MYSTICS
KNOWING NOTHING ABOUT LIMITATION
AND UNREALISTIC STATISTICS
ALWAYS MAKING A CHOICE TO LISTEN TO OUR INNER VOICE

HONOURING MOTHER EARTH
PRESERVING HER WORTH
DEALING WITH HEALING
REVEALING THE INTEGRITY OF HUMANITY LIVING IN UNITY
THE CORE OF OUR TRUE IDENTITY
SACRED SISTERHOOD & BROTHERHOOD

I HAD A VISION THAT OUR MISSION IS TO MAKE A DECISION
TO LIVE IN THE REALM OF REALITY
BY BEING TRUE TO OUR DIVINITY
IN EVERY ASPECT OF OUR LIVITY

# I HAD A VISION OF OUR TRUE ORIGIN. . .

THIS POEM IS INSPIRED BY THE PRINCIPLE OF ONENESS
KNOWN IN HINDU GREETING AS *"NAMASTE"*
– I AM YOU AND YOU ARE ME

IN MY NATIVE LANGUAGE OF SETSWANA IT IS KNOWN AS
*"BOTHO"*

IN ISIZULU IT IS KNOWN AS
*"UBUNTU"*
– I AM BECAUSE YOU ARE

IN THE RASTAFARIAN LIVITY IT IS KNOWN AS
*"I & I"*
IT IS THE PRINCIPLE OF 1 LOVE

IN CHRISTIANITY IT IS KNOWN AS
*"BROTHERLY LOVE"* OR *"CHRISTNESS"*

THESE WORDS SPEAK TO THE SACRED UNITY & INTEGRITY OF
HUMANITY
IT IS WHAT I BELIEVE TO BE OUR HIGHEST & TRUEST
EXPRESSION.
KINDNESS IS THE SIMPLEST WAY TO REVEAL WHO WE REALLY
ARE.
MANKIND AND WOMANKIND'S TRUE ESSENSE IS KINDNESS
MY VISION IS OF THAT MOMENT WHEN WE EACH AWAKEN TO THE
REALITY OF OUR DIVINITY.

# DEAR TECHNOLOGY

DEAR TECHNOLOGY
Y CAN'T YOU ERRADICATE POVERTY?
YOU'VE GOT AN APP FOR THIS & AN APP FOR THAT
YOU'VE BASICALLY GOT AN APP TO FIND ANY MAP
YOU'VE EVEN GOT THE CYBER POWER
TO BRIDGE THE COMMUNICATION GAP
BETWEEN PEOPLE IN DIFFERENT CONTINENTS
BUT
NO APP FOR FREE MOSQUITO NETS
OR AN APP TO CURE
THESE RUTHLESS WAR-DRIVEN MIND SETS
NO APP TO DEAL WITH SUICIDAL ATTEMPTS
NO APP TO ERASE MODERN MAN'S COUNTLESS
REGRETS

STILL
I GUESS YOU CAN'T TAKE ALL THE BLAME
FOR THE SOCIO-POLITICAL MIND GAME
THAT LABELS US WITH DIFFERENT NAMES
AND MAKES US THINK WE'RE NOT THE SAME

YET
SOMEHOW I THINK YOU DO ASSIST
IN WEAKENING OUR ABILITY TO RESIST
YOUR ENDLESS MINDLESS EGO TRIPS
BY MESMERIZING US WITH ADVERTISING
AIMED AT FEEDING OUR VAIN SENSATIONS
THAT UPHOLD OUR NARROW PERCEPTIONS
WHILE SIMULTANEOUSLY DISTRACTING US
FROM OUR MORAL OBLIGATIONS
AS WE COMPLACENTLY ENGAGE
IN YOUR LATEST INVENTIONS

LEAVING US NO TIME AND SPACE
FOR SPIRITUAL REFLECTIONS

OR
DO WE JUST USE YOU AS A SCAPEGOAT
SO WE CAN AVOID LOOKING WITHIN US
FOR THE ANTEDOTE
THAT WILL REVERSE THIS CURSE
OF QUICK FAST AND INSTANT
WHILE WE CONTINUE TO BECOME DISTANT
UNABLE TO FEEL EACH OTHERS PAIN
ENVIOUS OF EACH OTHERS GAIN
ANXIETY RIDDLED, CHRONIC CONSUMERS
IGNORING OUR GROWING ROBOTIC TUMOURS
PREFERING TO STARE AT OUR COMPUTER SCREENS
LIKE TROUBLED, HORMONAL TEENS
WE SIT THERE LATENT, BORED
& MENTALLY *VACANT*
TRYING TO HIDE OUR SOCIAL AILMENT
BY DENYING THE TRUTH THAT IS SO BLATENT

MAYBE
ONE DAY YOU'LL ADVANCE SO FAST
& TRANSPORT US BACK TO OUR ANCIENT PAST
WHERE WE WON'T HAVE TO HIDE
BEHIND THIS ILLUSIVE MASK
FREE FROM APPROVAL-ADDICTION

NO LONGER EXPOSING OURSELVES
TO YOUR HIGH RADIATION
THAT'S CONSTANTLY INTERFERING
WITH OUR NATURAL VIBRATION
TURNING US INTO ZOMBIE-LIKE SLAVES OF
STAGNATION

TRAPPING US IN YOUR CAGE
OF SCIENTIFIC EXPLOITATION
INSISTING ON CONTROL
BY MERE SPECULATION
FOR THE SOLE ADVANCEMENT
OF YOUR GREED DRIVEN CORPORATIONS
AIMED AT KEEPING US FROM ENGAGING
IN SPIRITUAL COMMUNICATIONS


PERHAPS
IN REALITY
U REALLY AREN'T THE MAIN CAUSE
FOR THIS INSANITY
WE ARE FACED WITH IN THE 21ST CENTURY
MARRIED TO CURRENCY
DIVORCED FROM INTEGRITY
DEPENDANT ON THE PHARMACEUTICAL INDUSTRY
THAT'S FOREVER CREATING MENTAL ILLNESSES
TO KEEP US IN OUR MISERY
WHILE WE STAY RELIANT ON MACHINERY
INSTEAD OF HEALING OUR HEARTS INTERNALLY


SO
I'M LEFT QUESTIONING YOUR MECHANICAL SPELL
THAT'S CAUSING US TO LIVE
IN THIS TECHNICAL HELL
TOO HOOKED TO SUDDENLY REBEL
AFRAID TO FACE THE FACT
THAT YOU ARE JUST AN EFFECT
OF OUR PERSONAL DEFECT
REFUSING TO ADMIT
THAT WE ARE A PART OF WHAT WE CREATE
HENCE WE ARE UNABLE TO RETALIATE
BY SPITTING OUT YOUR WIRELESS BAIT

COZ YOU SOMEHOW MANAGE TO MANIPULATE
CAPTIVATE AND THEN INTEROGATE
US BY TELLING US TO
CLICK ON A LINK
THEN DEEPER & DEEPER
INTO YOUR TRAP WE SINK
UNTIL WE R UNABLE TO BLINK
YET STILL
I DON'T THINK
I HOLD A VALID CASE
SINCE YOU ARE A PRODUCT OF US
- THE HUMAN RACE -
AND YOUR ONLY CRIME
IS CUNNINGLY STEALING OUR VALUABLE TIME
KEEPING US FROM LOOKING WITHIN US
FOR THE ANTI-VIRUS THAT WILL ULTIMATELY FREE US.

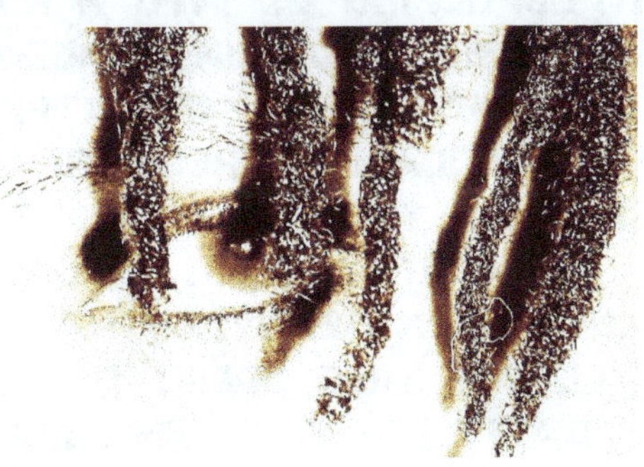

# DEAR TECHNOLOGY – EXPLANATION:

I WROTE THIS PARTICULAR POEM WHEN I REALIZED
JUST HOW MUCH TIME & MONEY WE SPEND ON
TECHNOLOGY. HOW RELIANT WE ARE ON IT AND HOW
QUICKLY IT IS GROWING ON US, YET WITH ALL ITS
SPEEDY ADVANCEMENT, I QUESTIONED WHETHER IT IS
BEING USED TO ITS FULL POTENTIAL TO SOLVE THE
PROBLEMS THAT AFFLICT THE LARGER PERCENTAGE OF
HUMANITY THAT CANNOT ACCESS IT.
IF SUCH A MASSIVE LEAP INTO THE FUTURE CANNOT
FEED THE POOR, CURE THE SICK, MEND THE
BROTHERHOOD OF MAN OR SIMPLY PUT AN END TO
WAR, THEN MY QUESTION IS WHETHER TECHNOLOGY IS
REALLY AIDING IN OUR COLLECTIVE EVOLUTION OR IS
IT DEVOLVING US INTO A ROBOTIC, ISOLATED SPECIES,
FOREVER SEEKING VALIDATION, APPROVAL AND
ANSWERS FROM AN EXTERNAL FORCE INSTEAD OF
LOCATING THE SPIRITUAL SOURCE WITHIN.
I REACH THE CONCLUSION THAT TECHNOLOGY IS OUR
INVENTION SO IT IS UP TO US TO CHECK OUR
MOTIVATIONS & INTENTIONS & TO QUESTION WHETHER
ALL THE TIME SPENT ON PROFILE PICTURES, STATUS
UPDATES, UPLOADS AND DOWNLOADS, LIKES, INBOXES,
POKES & FRIEND REQUESTS, IS HELPING US EVOLVE IN
LOVE OR DEVOLVE INTO VAIN, IMAGE-DRIVEN CHRONIC
CONSUMERS. IN ADDRESSING TECHNOLOGY, I FOUND
MYSELF AUTOMATICALLY ADDRESSING THE
TECHNICALLY VULNERABLE PART OF MYSELF.
SO IN ACTUALITY I AM PART OF TECHNOLOGY
IN WHICHEVER WAY I CHOOSE TO BE,
NEGATIVELY OR POSITIVELY.
ITS ALL UP TO US SINCE WE ARE ALL A PART OF
WHAT WE IMPART.

# LIVING WORDS

LIGHT SHINES OUT OF DARKNESS
WHAT YOU REAP IS WHAT YOU SOW
- THIS YOU HAVE TO KNOW!
YOU ARE THE SUM TOTAL OF WHAT YOU THINK
THINK POSITIVE THOUGHTS
- GOOD THINGS - PURE THINGS
RISE TO THIS TASK
THROW AWAY THE MASK
BE YOURSELF
MAKE TIME
TO BE STILL WITHIN

DON'T LIVE YOUR LIFE
ON A TREADMILL, RUSHING TO NOWHERE
BE AWARE,
MINDFULL, ALWAYS MINDFULL
DANCE FREE – KULULEKA [KULU-LEH-GA]
LAUGH FREE – PUTULUHA [PUDU-LU-HA]
LOVE FREE - SMILE FREE – CXANULUHA [CLICK!ANULUHA]
FREELY WE RECEIVE
SO THEN FREELY WE GIVE
SO THAT WE CAN ALL FREELY LIVE

NEVER FORGET ABOUT FORGIVENESS
IT WILL FREE YOU FROM MADNESS
LOOK DEEP WITHIN YOURSELF
INSIDE THERE'S A KEY
TO SELF-EVOLUTION, SELF-REALIZATION
BE CONSCIOUS OF ONENESS, TENDERNESS N KINDNESS
TIMELESS THOUGHTS OF REALITY
BEAUTY SHINES FROM INTEGRITY
INTEGRITY STEMS FROM LIVING IN LOVE
THE REASON FOR OUR EXISTENCE
OUR SPIRITUAL INSURANCE

OBSERVE YOURSELF LOVINGLY,
LEARN WITH HUMILITY
ABOUT YOUR UNIVERSAL SURROUNDINGS
REMEMBER EARTH IS NOT WHERE YOU ORIGINATE
– YOU ARE NOT JUST A BODY –
YOUR VOICE ECHOES THROUGHOUT THE COSMOS
YOU ARE AN EXPRESSION OF INFINITE INTELLIGENCE
LIMITLESS MIND OF THE ALLMIGHTY "I AM" PRINCIPLE
BEYOND SCIENCE – MULTI DIMENSIONAL SPIRIT BEING
DYNAMIC MANIFESTATION – INDESTRUCTIBLE ENERGY
EVER GROWING
EVER CHANGING
EVER EVOLVING
NEVER DISSOLVING
COMPACT POWER UNLEASHED
BRIGHTER THAN THE SUN RAY
NO NEED TO HIDE YOUR LIGHT AWAY
THIS IS A NEW DAY, SEE YOURSELF IN A TRUE WAY
MOULD YOUR DREAMS LIKE CLAY
SAY WHAT YOU WERE BORN TO SAY

KHABI'S FIRST LIVE POETRY READING, WOA! ART GALLERY, 3/5/14

# THE LOVE I LONGED TO KNOW

I often ask myself y you gave me up
When I needed you the most
I patiently awaited your return
As the days turned into weeks -
Weeks into months - months into years
Each phase n stage riddled with endless questions
Like
What made u give up on me?
What made you stay away?
As special moments passed away
Without leaving any special memories -
Memories I'd longed to share with you
Yet
Even during our brief contact
I often wondered if you felt the same -
If you ever missed me or if you wanted me at all

I watched childhood hopes turn into wishes
Wishes into tears
Tears into prayers
Prayers into a string of more
Urgent questions

As a teen I rebelled
In an attempt to block the hurt
Of abandonment I was hiding in my heart
I became an expert
At quietly clearing your name
And taking the blame
As a militant aim to cover up the shame
Of holding on to a dream I now saw as lame
Deep down inside
I still longed for your love to make me sane again
The endless questions were fast
Becoming a flaming strain
Thru courage n grace
I grew up n grew strong through all that pain
The stronger part of me accepted my fate
I still didn't believe it was too late
So I gave you a chance to prove yourself
And maybe make me understand
Maybe you were just a victim of the unkind system
That turned you against yourself n everything
That came from you

But what gets me twisted is how you managed
To fill me with so much guilt
For simply asking y u left
As if I had no right to know!

I tried to look past the past
And gave you a second chance

Only this time I hoped my quest would be laid to rest
By putting myself to the test
I convinced myself that maybe
If I showed you all the love you never showed me
You would understand my humble plea

I gave n gave
And I even let you take freely
Without a second thought
B'coz
The little girl in me
Still wanted to please you
To make you proud
I just couldn't let her down
She still longed for your approval
Your affection n your undivided attention
To listen, to cuddle
To understand her struggle
She longed for you to take the opportunity
To give some sort of heart-felt apology
Or simply take responsibility
If not for leaving then for not coming back
She longed for you
To accept her - to love n nurture her
Or
To just set her free from all the questioning

Time being no time waster
She watched it swiftly passing by

Your presence
Left her with as many questions as
Your absence
And no matter how hard she tries n tried
She could no longer force you to bond with her
Maybe, just maybe it's just one of those things
That were just not meant to be
- Or maybe
The easiest answer is
Acceptance of what is and what will never be
Maybe all I need
Is to claim back a piece of my peace
In the higher wisdom
That's always guiding me, reminding me
That the earthly love I longed for
Was the Divine Love alive in me
This is all the strength I need to set you free
from the questioning part of me!!!!
I Forgive myself for being a prisoner
To what was never meant for me!!

# THE LOVE I LONGED TO KNOW

Poetry has always been my form of personal therapy so when I wrote *"The love I longed to know"* it was my way of airing out the toxic emotional baggage I had carried with me throughout childhood into adulthood. The fermented feelings were automatically bubbling over and leaking into every aspect of my life so I came to a point where I could no longer block it out or make it an excuse. The moment I took responsibility and addressed the fear & sadness that was hiding within the anger I felt and expressed, was the moment I found strength, healing, understanding and forgiveness within myself. As a result I was able to gradually let go of the pain. The best part of the whole journey was that I was able to give forgiveness and show a genuine level of understanding and acceptance of what was, what is and what will never be. My hope is that this expression of me inspires you to face the issues within you that have kept you from finding healing, forgiveness, understanding and closure.


(UNFORGIVENESS, RESENTMENT, ANGER & FEAR
ARE SCIENTIFICALLY PROVEN TO CAUSE ILLNESS &
CAN HINDER YOU FROM BEING
THE HIGHEST EXPRESSION OF YOU)
- MAKE TIME & TAKE TIME TO INVEST IN YOU -
HEAL YOURSELF, FORGIVE YOURSELF, UNDERSTAND
YOURSELF & KNOW YOURSELF

# Ode to the Highest

("Kea leboga" [*ghee-a lebokha*], "Asante" & "Enkosi" [ing-gosi]
mean "thank you" in Setswana, Swahili & Xhosa [click!osa])


Kea leboga
for showing me the Beauty in All seasons, in All chapters and
in All things.
From abandonment I have harnessed the courage to stand
strong and walk my path.
From hardship I have learnt the beauty of patient endurance.
From tearful days n nights I have learnt the beauty of pouring
out emotion instead of harbouring grudges n holding on to
toxic feelings.
From organised religion I have learnt the importance of
mastering myself  instead of allowing some1 less experienced
in the art of me insisting on mastering me.
The beautiful lesson learnt is freedom of being.
From growing up in racial segregation
I have learnt that unearned white or black privilege is the
blinding enemy that poisons the human soul.

The beauty I grasped is to live integrally with integrity
and never let hate dictate the way.
From depression I have learnt that even dark emotions seek
observation & expression not repression. I have learnt that at
these low times the soul is working its magic, filling us with
new light and new life.
Tenderness is a gift from pain.
From being labelled a bloody foreigner in the West
I have learnt that it's a compliment to be reminded of the
blood of the Ancient Mystics that runs through my veins
who hail from the land of the Rising Sun.
While the birds n the bees,  the Seas n the Trees,
the music of the wind and the look of Love in Kindred Spirits
are a constant reminder
that I AM ONE with ALL of Mother Earth
EAST * WEST * NORTH n SOUTH
are my heritage and habitat.
The Beauty I grasped is that no one is a foreigner,
it's just another illusion
used by the deluded.
From my Ancestors
I have learned of resilience, tenderness & tolerance
the Power of Infinite Love and Infinite Light of Beingness
in body * in soul * n in Spirit
Asante to the Highest
for the privilege to find n express
the Highest WithIn Myself
the Beauty to Rise after every fall
to Smile, to Dance, to Laugh, to Write, to Love and be Loved
Enkosi to the Highest;
Supreme OverSoul of the Diverse Universe.

# THE MENTAL CAGE IN STAGES

## (THINK YOURSELF FREE
## LIKE THE BIRDS IN THE TREES)

The first stage in the mental cage is deceit
blinding those who are self obsessed
who describe themselves as elite
unaware they are slaves
who are bound by the chains of ignorance
victims of vanity & arrogance
mistaking restless activity for creativity
pinned down by greedy demands
of unrealistic, materialistic expectations
false pride pulling the reins of their mind
They have forgotten
that the essence of mankind is to be kind
Moving in circles in a mental cage
where the blind are leading the blind

afraid to step down off their non-existent pedestal
completely unaware that their disease is mental


The next stage in the mental cage is confusion
Masses trapped by selfish ambitions
shifting swiftly from illusion to delusion
believing in some form of national security
while neglecting to address their inner wars & insecurities
many betraying their humanity
driving themselves to insanity
afraid to step down from their own high class opinion
completely unaware that their illness is mental


The third stage in the mental cage is inner rage
Shackled by turmoil and spiritual drought
riddled with fear and self doubt
going round and round on life's roundabout
aware that you are part of a mind game
but not completely sure who to blame
you've tasted a hint of shame
because
by questioning you are considered insane
by the status quo who simply don't want to know
completely unaware that they are being ignorant
of a mental ailment that is keeping them stagnant


By questioning you are breaking Free from the cage
you are aware – becoming vigilant

with each question you are
making a life–changing choice to listen to your inner voice


The Source of Light
is presenting You with the perfect opportunity
to live in the Reality of your Liberty – as Divine Entity
to BREAK FREE & BE all that you were Created to BE
The mental cage is just a reminder
that
only You can emancipate yourself
at any stage of Mental Slavery
You are your own redemption
You are your own salvation
the Kingdom is WithIn You –
Let Nothing extinguish the Fire Burning in Your Soul

47

# THE MENTAL CAGE IN STAGES

## – EXPLANATION:

This poem is inspired by the legendary Bob Marley in Redemption Song: the lyrics have always resonated deep within me, especially when he sings the verse, "Emancipate yourselves from mental slavery, none but ourselves can free our minds".

I wrote *"The Mental Cage In Stages"* because we evolve in stages. There are stages where we feel trapped by some ideology, creed, dogma or some false belief simply because we are afraid to break free from the crowd and pave our own path.

We choose to remain in the cage because it's what everyone else seems to do, meanwhile deep within our souls there's a yearning for self realization; self discovery that seems to conflict with the principles in the cage.

The day I broke free, it was nothing like a fairytale. Many times when my own freedom put me to the test, all I wanted to do was run back to the safety of the cage.

Liberty requires responsibility but it is all an inside job into getting to know yourself fully by enjoying shining your light but also accepting the shadows that are cast by your own light. Its all about balance.

Needless to say after many years of being trapped in certain patterns of thinking, it takes a lot to break free but nothing is worse than being trapped in a mental cage of narrow mindedness, limited opinion or unexplored possibilities.

Only you can free your mind. No one knows how trapped you are except you. That feeling inside that knows there's more to life is the key to unlocking the cage and breaking free so you can be all that you were created to be.

Live your truth, there will be mistakes but that's just what freedom is all about. Walking your own journey, learning from your own mistakes.
Only you can be you!!!!

# UNITY IN DIVERSITY
(CO-WRITTEN BY JUDAH JAH LOVE)

I HAIL THE INFINITE CHRIST
YOU HAIL RASTAFARI
THE SAME SPIRIT OF LIFE

I LOOK FOR INSPIRATION IN THE WAYS OF BUDDHA
YOU LOOK INTO THE MYSTERIES OF ANCIENT EGYPT
OUR SEARCH BRINGS US TO THE SAME UNIVERSAL
SOURCE OF LIGHT WITHIN OURSELVES
DIVINE UNITY

YOU HAVE POETRY
I HAVE ART
IT'S ONE EXPRESSION
FOR POETRY IS ART
THE ANCIENT EGYPTIANS ARE BUDDHAS
RASTAFARI IS CHRIST
DIVINE UNITY
IS EVERYWHERE IN EVERYTHING

IN A MIRROR YOU FIND YOU
I FIND ME
I *AM* YOU
DIVINE UNITY
ONENESS
ALL ONE IN GOD

# WAKE UP

STOP HIDING BEHIND YOUR MAKE UP
YOU'VE WALLOWED TOO LONG IN YOUR HANG UPS
MAYBE IT'S TIME FOR YOU TO STAND UP
AND TAKE RESPONSIBILITY FOR YOUR MESS UPS
THE TRUTH YOU KNOW WITHIN IS PROOF ENOUGH
THAT YOU CAN RISE UP AND SHAKE OFF
ALL OF THE DUST FROM YOUR PAST
YOU HAVE TO FULFILL YOUR HIGHER TASK
SO NOW YOU MUST THROW AWAY THAT MASK

# STOP !!!

- TREATING THE EFFECTS OF YOUR DEFECTS
- LOOK WITHIN AND LOCATE THE REAL CAUSE OF YOUR
FLAWS AND HEAVY REGRETS
YOU'LL OFTEN FIND THAT THE ROOT OF THAT BITTER FRUIT
IS EMBEDDED IN A CARELESS THOUGHT
THAT CREPT SILENTLY WITHIN YOUR MIND
AT A TIME WHEN YOU WERE BEING UNKIND
- OPEN YOUR 3RD EYE – REFUSE TO BE BLIND
- LIVE LIFE FROM THE INSIDE OUT
- DON'T BE SWAYED BY FEAR N DOUBT
- LOVE DEEPLY FROM THE VERY DEPTH OF YOUR HEART
KNOWING THAT YOU WILL ALWAYS BE A PART OF WHAT YOU
IMPART
WHAT YOU REAP IS WHAT YOU SOW
SO
LET YOUR
SEEDS OF KINDNESS GROW
THEN LOVE, JOY & HARMONY
ON EARTH WILL REIGN AND OVERFLOW

# INFINITE LOVELIGHT

LOVELIGHT SHINE BRIGHT
LEAD ME INTO DIVINE INSIGHT
TEACH ME TO DISCERN WHAT'S WRONG FROM WHAT'S RIGHT
SATISFY MY SPIRITUAL APPETITE
GUIDE ME TO THE PLACE OF TRUE DELIGHT
FILL ME WITH INNER BLISS
LET ME NEVER GO AMISS
FROM YOUR PERFECT WILL
KEEP ME STRONG AND STILL
EVEN IN THE DARKEST NIGHT AND HARDEST PLIGHT
HELP ME HOLD TIGHT TO YOUR INFINITE MIGHT
THAT I MAY REACH THE HIGHEST HEIGHT
THAT ALWAYS LEADS ME DEEPER INTO
INFINITE LOVELIGHT

# KARA BOPHELO ASHENAFI ABREY

OVERWHELMING JOY FLOODED MY WHOLE BEING

THE MOMENT YOUR SPIRIT CHOSE US

JAH LOVE SAID A PRAYER AS YOU WERE CONCEIVED

GIVING THANKHS N PRAISE TO THE MOST HIGH

& THE HIGHEST CREATOR

GOD N GODDESS

FOR THE PRECIOUS GIFT OF NEW LIFE – BOPHELO –

BESTOWED UPON US.

ON

7TH OF 12TH MONTH

THRU MODERN TEGHNOLOGY

WE LISTENED TO YOUR HEART BEAT

IT REMINDED ME OF THE DRUM BEAT

IN THE LAND OF THE RISING SUN

THE NUBIAN SOUNDS OF KA & RA

RESONATED WITHIN ME

REPRESENTING THE INFINITE

SPIRIT OF THE RISING SUN.

AND TO YOUR FATHER

(YOU ARE) THE SYMBOL OF THE ANKH

INFINITE LIFE

HE SAID YOU ARE

ASHENAFI

A MIGHTY CONQUEROR

YOU ARE THE PERFECT SYMBOL

OF THE SPECIAL UNION BETWEEN LOVE, LIGHT N BLISS

ETERNITY HAS BLESSED US WITH PURE BEING

KARA BOPHELO ASHENAFI

A GIFT OF UNITY.

16TH OF 2ND MONTH

A STRONG BEAUTIFUL PRINCESS IS WITH US

NO WORDS CAN DESCRIBE THAT

PRICELESS MOMENT

THANKH YOU FOR CHOOSING US

***KARA (INFINITE SPIRIT OF THE RADIANT SUN)**

***BOPHELO (LIFE)**

***ASHENAFI (CONQUEROR)**

***ABREY**

– EXPLANATION BY JUDAH JAH LOVE:


HERE, KHABI DOCUMENTS THE DATE WE FIRST HEARD OUR BABY'S HEARTBEAT AND THE DATE WE FOUND OUT WE WERE HAVING A DAUGHTER – JUST AS WE WANTED AND HAD ALREADY MADE A LONG LIST OF NAMES FOR.


WE BOTH LOVED THE NAME, "KARA", WHICH WE MADE UP OF THE ANCIENT EGYPTIAN WORDS, "KA", MEANING SPIRIT, AND "RA", THE DIVINE SUN.

DURING ONE OF MANY NAME-BRAINSTORMS, I ASKED KHABI WHAT THE WORD FOR "LIFE" IS IN HER MOTHER-TONGUE, SETSWANA; IT'S, "BOPHELO" [*BOH-PEE-LOH*]. I LOVED IT. I INSTANTLY NICKNAMED HER, "BOPHI".

"ASHENAFI" IS AN AMHARIC (ETHIOPIAN – HENCE THE PICTURE OF THE CROSS-SHAPED ETHIOPIAN CHURCH) WORD THAT MEANS, "CONQUEROR".

"ABREY" IS OUR SURNAME, WHICH COMES FROM THE NAME "ABRAHAM".

# LOVE LOVED ME
## (LOVE IS THE SOURCE OF ALL RESOURCES)

LOVE LOVED ME FREE
RELEASED ME FROM MENTAL SLAVERY
LOVE LOVED ME BE
UNLEASHING THE HIGHEST IN ME
LOVE LOVED ME UNCONDITIONALLY
ELEVATING ME SPIRITUALLY
LOVE LOVED ME WISELY
TEACHING & REVEALING
TIMELESS MYSTERIES
LOVE LOVED ME PROTECTIVELY
LEADING, SHIELDING
& GUIDING ME
LOVE LOVED ME
THROUGH EVERY SITUATION
GRANTING ME
STILLNESS & INSPIRATION
LOVE LOVED ME WITH PURITY
HELPING ME ACCEPT MY COMPLEXITY
LOVE LOVED ME
WIPING AWAY EVERY TEAR CAUSED BY FEAR
LOVE LOVED ME TRULY
UNVEILING MY SACRED IDENTITY
SHOWING ME THE BEAUTY OF MY DIVINITY
LOVE LOVED ME FOR FREE
UNLEASHING THE HIGHEST WITHIN ME.

# FORGET THE SHADOWS

ALL THE SHADOWS THAT MAKE YOU CRY
ALL THE SHADOWS THAT MAKE YOU SIGH
ALL THE SHADOWS THAT SEEM SO REAL
ALL THE SHADOWS THAT WE CONCEAL
ALL THE SHADOWS THAT WAGE A WAR
ALL THE SHADOWS THAT RAGE & ROAR
ALL THE SHADOWS THAT INTIMIDATE
ALL THE SHADOWS THAT MANIPULATE

THESE DREADFUL SHADOWS THAT FRIGHTEN KINGS
HIDEOUS SHADOWS THAT MAGNIFY THINGS
ALL THESE SHADOWS THAT OPPOSE OUR INNER PEACE
SHADOWS THAT FIGHT AGAINST OUR DIVINE INCREASE
THESE SHADOWS DEMAND OUR SANITY
THESE SHADOWS WANNA CLAIM OUR DIGNITY
THESE SHADOWS WANT A FIGHT
THESE SHADOWS AIM TO DIM OUR LIGHT
HOW, THEN, DO WE FACE THESE VICIOUS TYRANTS
THAT SEEK TO FOREVER TORMENT OUR SPIRIT
HOW DO WE SILENCE THIS VOICE OF VIOLENCE

THE STAKES ARE HIGH
THE RISKS SEEM CERTAIN
OUR SURE DEFENCE IS WITHIN
FOR ONLY WHEN WE SHINE OUR INNER LIGHT
DIRECTLY ON THESE SHADOWS DO

WE SEE THEM FADE AWAY INTO THE NOTHINGNESS
FROM WHICH THEY CAME

WE SLOWLY BEGIN TO REALIZE THAT
THESE DARK FIGURES ARE JUST
FIGMENTS OF NEGATIVE IMAGINATIONS
HIDDEN IN NEGATIVE THOUGHT PATTERNS
OF FEAR
**BUT**
WHEN WE STAND IN THE LIGHT OF TRUTH
THEY IMMEDIATELY DISINTEGRATE
**FOR PERFECT LOVE CASTS AWAY FEAR**

**NOW**
**IS THE BEST TIME**
TO OPEN UP
OUR 3RD EYE & TO LIVE IN THE DIVINE REVELATION
THAT OUR SPIRIT KNOWS NO LIMITS
SO THESE SHADOWS R FAKE
THEY ARE AN ILLUSION, A STAGED DELUSION
IT'S ALL A SHAM
WE R THE INDESTRUCTIBLE SEED OF ABRAHAM
THESE
SHADOWS HAVE NO REALITY
AND CERTAINLY NO PLACE
IN OUR DIVINITY

**I & I ARE INFINITE LIGHT BEING !!!!**

# & THEN
# FEAR HAPPENED TO MAKE US FORGET
# YET LOVE IS ALWAYS THE GUIDING LIGHT

At first we were free
Just to simply be
We laughed out loud
We were not bound
With dreams big & bright
Nothing could dim our light
We danced with no restraint
We didn't entertain strain
We told our stories warmly
We expressed ourselves boldly
We wore our melanin cloak with dignity
Unashamed of our identity

## & THEN
## FEAR HAPPENED TO MAKE US FORGET

At first we forgot all about our divinity
Which led us to forget our humanity
We forgot about our inner strength
The true treasure of our worth
We forgot how the stars announced our birth
We forgot we are sons & daughters of Mama Earth
We forgot to tell our story
Of timeless glory

We forgot about our oneness – unity & integrity
We forgot about our ancient bond of solidarity
We forgot all, how to dance & free lance
We forgot about our dreams
& found ourselves in dire crime scenes
We forgot about sisterhood & brotherhood
Removed from nature then placed in the hood
Forgot that melanin is our cloak of pride

So we used it to our shame
Which brought us pain & increased our strain
We forgot that in our culture
Death only ever meant rebirth
A transformation into higher dimensions
& so we lost our direction

We forgot we had a choice
We forgot to listen to our inner voice
YET WE MUST NEVER FORGET THAT
FEAR HAPPENED TO TEACH US THE LESSONS OF PAIN -
FEAR CAME TO REMIND US NEVER TO PUSH LOVE AWAY
For in the cycles of evolution
Perfect LOVE casts away fear
Only love can restore our foundations
Only love can bring liberation
Only love can raise our vibration
Fear is the yin
Love is the yang
Manifesting balance
Love is the master
The totality of all reality
When love happens, fear fades away

# INNER DE SANCTUARY

INNER DE SANCTUARY OF I HEART
I SEE US AS I
I SEE I LIFTING FROM ILLUSION
I SEE I RISING FROM CONFUSION
I SEE I SOARING HIGH BEYOND THE SKY

INNER DE SANCTUARY OF I MIND
I SEE I REASONING WITH  STAR BEINGS
I SEE I IN THE SACRED DIMENSIONS
WITH CRYSTAL CLEAR EYE SIGHT
RADIATING AN INFINTE LIGHT SO BRIGHT

INNER DE SANCTUARY OF I SOUL
I SEE I & I WHOLE
IN 1NESS
THE NEW DAWNING OF CHRIST CONSCIOUSNESS
THE CROWN OF I DIVINITY
REFLECTED IN THE TOTALITY
OF I PRESENT REALITY

# DANCE

DANCE
FOR THE HEALING OF ALL NATIONS
& GENERATIONS
DANCE TO RAISE
POSITIVE VIBRATIONS
DANCE FOR EASE
DANCE FOR RELEASE
DANCE FOR THE INCREASE
OF INNER PEACE


[Unfinished]

# FREE

FREE FROM YOUR DOGMA AND CREEDS
FREE FROM YOUR INSATIABLE GREED
FREE FROM YOUR SNARES
FREE FROM YOUR CARES

**[Unfinished]**

# BOKHABINYANA
# RADIANCE LOVELIGHT

— KNYSNA, SOUTH AFRICA, 2012

# GIVING THANKHS

[Notes to Julia, Mangwane, Mom, One Love, Keety & Tabz, sis Simiah & Jah Free, Thandi, Biggie (Kguwi), Lefa & KaRa are from Khabi's un-finished "Thankh You's"]

Father-God/Mother-Goddess for Life, Love & Blessingz.
Tata [*Dada*] Madiba - Nelson Mandela - enkosi for freedom.
Mama Afreeka for history, culture & knowledge.
My Precious Jewel (Julia Khumalo aka Mocha Aunty Madlisa) ~ for turning every complexity into simplicity by bringing humour into every situation. With you ~ I never face the danger of taking myself too seriously & getting too stuffy. YOUR FRIENDSHIP IS HEALING N REFRESHING* THANK YOU 4 BEING (Bcoz u r I am)
Mangwane ~ Priceless Sistahood ~ My source of reference for ~ Botho~Ubuntu ~ my guaranteed support system ~ driving hours with the kids to rescue me from my pregnant hormones into the countryside for much needed rest ~ a fresh perspective n going out of your way to make sure I had the smoothest pregnancy, knowing
how to make me relax n smile! Hottest Godmother.
Mom in law ~ where to begin... You r Absolutely Amazing!!!!!
Driving me to all my appointments waiting for hours ~ unlistable support thru the driest season (lol) You r an awesome Mom, Nana Friend and make up supplier. Lol
One Love Foundation ~ Know your rootz Family ~ supporting us by buying the book n jewellery at dances ~ showering us with kindness ~ musical healing that allowed us to dance

thru da storm. U make 1ness a reality.
Thank you All so much.
Keety, Tabitha n family ~ laughter ~ meals ~ friendship ~
music, comedy ~ lifts ~ vibes & a memorable 30th.
Sis Simiah n Jah Free, nice vibes.
Thandi ~ letting me moan n moan* supportive sista
Biggie ~ sending home, Mzansi to me ~ music ~ comedy ~
dvds, gets me thru da cold days, makes me feel warm inside
Lefa ~ proving the resilience of da champion bloodline*
Kamo, for what u said to me that night, it means so much to
me. U r the best niece anyone could wish 4! X
My lion king, Judah, thankh u 4 Jah Love
& 4 KaRa (Jah Life). X
KaRa, thankh u 4 choosing us – I love the way u move! X
Mommy, Baringe, Malume, Mme Motswadi & Sakie:
Bcoz of u, I am. X
Chomaliza n Presh, kea leboga 4 always truly being there
for me. X; Janne (Jahson & Anne), Shaun n family for da
love. X; Poshi, Lesedi Light, Nomsa, Kamo, Palesa n family,
Romeo n Cynthia, queen Shammel n Ara, sis Kay n Motheo,
sis Karin n family, sis Leah n family, sis Kerri, Carlz, aus
Puse, aus Tiny, ma Juks, Kebra n Mamsey, Tshepi n family,
Promise, Thuli, Tebogo, Azania n Ruby, Roddie, Zulu, Carine,
Lydia, Bheki, Xoli, Gaz, Betty, Professor, John, Azania
Zulu, Sisa, Charlotte, Aminata, Sarah, Vuye, Mpume, Lindo,
Mafanyolle (my Gemini), Clive, Derry, Adelle, Johnny,
Tempa, Sara, Mirie, Jimmy, Barber n Precious, Sabi
& many more... Love n Blessingz to u All!

X